DogFish

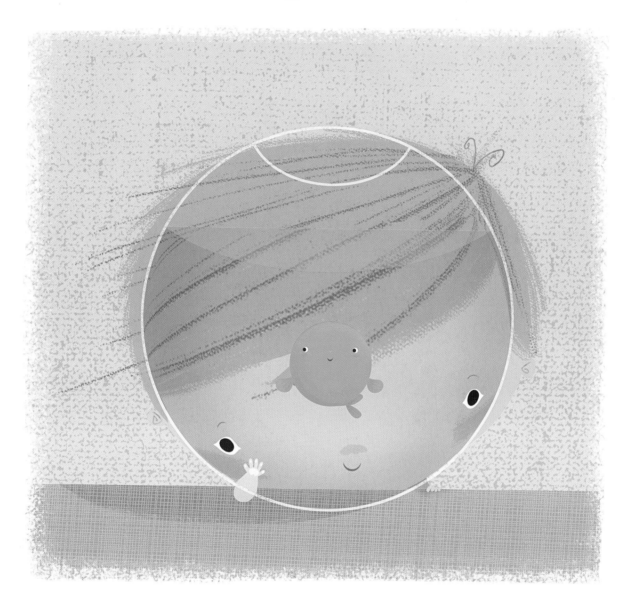

Gillian Shields

Illustrated by Dan Taylor

SIMON AND SCHUSTER
London · New York · Sydney

Everyone has a dog . . .

except me.

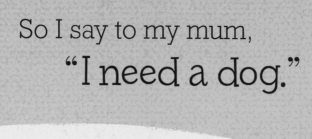

So I say to my mum,
"I need a dog."

But my mum says,

"Why do you need a dog when
you have such a nice goldfish?"

She always says things like that.

I explain that goldfish cannot . . .

catch sticks,

or go for walks,

or sit by your feet.

**And they NEVER
wag their tails.**

"That is why," I say, looking at her with my hypnotising eyes,

"I NEED A DOG."

But my mum says,
  "*We'll see*," which really means, "**NO.**"

I look sad.
  My goldfish looks sad too.

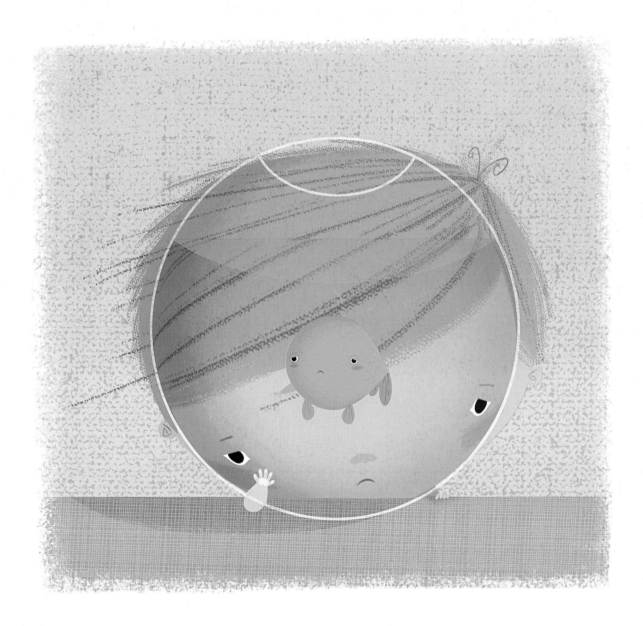

These are our sad looks.

So my mum says, in her kind-and-caring voice,
"But, honey, how could we have a dog
when we live on the forty-fourth floor?"

I think for a bit and say,
"Four hundred and forty-four
stairs would be very good
exercise for a dog."

Then she says, in her soothing-and-explaining voice,
"But, sweetheart, wouldn't the dog be bored
all day, when I'm at work and you're in school?"

So I think a bit more and say,
"It could read the paper?"

And my mum looks irritated but sorrowful. Like this.

Then she says, in her this-really-is-the-end-of-the-matter voice,
   "Now, darling, how could we possibly
   afford to feed a great big hungry dog?"

But I say, as quick as a fish,
"I don't want a big hungry dog. I want
a very, very, very small dog that eats
hardly anything at all. Just scraps."

Then we all look how people look when
The Situation is Hopeless. Like this.

After a bit, my mum says,
   "Well, if you can't have what you want,
   you could try to want what you have."

She ALWAYS says things like that.

So then I look at my goldfish.

And my goldfish looks at me
with his hypnotising eyes, and I think,

"Maybe . . . just maybe . . ."

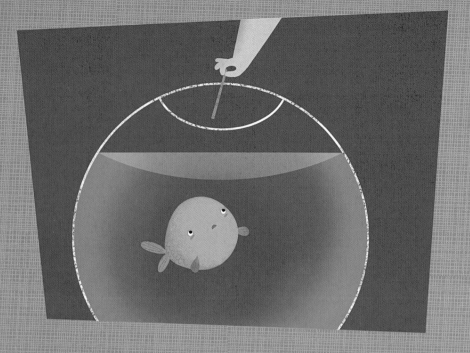

So I teach my goldfish to catch a teeny tiny stick.

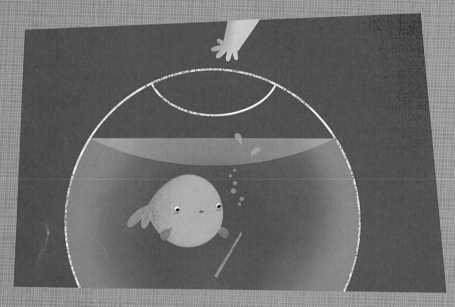

It takes practice.

It is a tough job.

Sometimes I think it is
A Waste of Time.

But we get there in the end – and it feels good!

This is how good it feels.

I take my goldfish for walks . . .

. . . and he takes me for walks.

We climb
the four hundred
and forty-four stairs –

together.

When we are out, he reads the paper.
He's never bored.

He
eats

hardly

anything

at all.

Just scraps.

In the evening, he sits by my feet,
and I tell him stuff. He's a great listener.

He can even wag his tail to say, "I love you."
He's not just a goldfish . . .

He's a DOGfish!

So now, when I see everyone with their ordinary old dogs, I say . . .

"Why would I need a dog when I
have the best goldfish in the world?"

I like saying that.

And I look, and my mum looks, and my goldfish looks utterly, totally, blissfully...

HAPPY!

Just like this.

THE END